For the *Love* of Golf

An A-to-Z Primer for Golf Fans of All Ages

Foreword by **Arnold Palmer**   *Written by* **Frederick C. Klein**   *Illustrated and Designed by* **Mark Anderson**

Foreword

The history of competitive golf in the United States goes back a little more than one hundred years, and it pleases me to realize that I've touched just about all of it in one way or another.

I was too young to have seen such early heroes as Francis Ouimet, Bobby Jones, and Gene Sarazen play, but as a boy I read about them and came to know them in later life. My career crossed briefly with those of Ben Hogan, Sam Snead, Byron Nelson, and Babe Didrikson Zaharias. I made a bit of history myself matching strokes with Jack Nicklaus, Lee Trevino, and others of my own generation. Now I can watch current stars like Tiger Woods, Phil Mickelson, and Vijay Singh and remember playing friendly rounds with them when they were getting started.

All of those people are in this book, which tells golf's story in rhyme, text, and wonderfully executed drawings. It's a story I think everyone will like, young people especially, and I'm proud to be part of it.

—Arnold Palmer

"A" is for St. Andrews,

Where Scotsmen with crooks Invented the game and Put rules on the books.

GAMES INVOLVING STICKS AND BALLS DATE TO ROMAN TIMES, but the one that evolved into the modern game of golf was developed by Scotsmen on the duneland along the North Sea near the city of Edinburgh. One of the earliest golfing groups was formed in the middle 18th century in the seaside town of St. Andrews. It became the Royal and Ancient Golf Club, which formulated the first set of rules for the sport in 1754 and administered them internationally for many years thereafter. The Old Course at St. Andrews, still the R&A's headquarters, is no mere relic. Lengthened to accommodate the modern game, it's one of a half dozen courses that take turns hosting the British Open, one of the sport's four annual major tournaments.

"B" is for Ballesteros,

Who sprayed many a drive,
But slashed out of the rough
To keep his hopes alive.

SEVERIANO BALLESTEROS is an ex-caddie from Pedrena, Spain, who sparked a European golf revival in the late seventies. He was often erratic off the tee, but his ability to scramble was legendary and helped him to win 65 tournaments worldwide, including three British Opens (in 1979, 1984, and 1988) and two Masters (in 1980 and 1983). A fierce competitor, he led the European team to parity with the United States in the Ryder Cup, golf's premier international team event.

Another European golfer making a strong mark on the game is ANIKA SORENSTAM, from Sweden. She's the best female player of the current era. She has won the Ladies Professional Golf Association's (LPGA) Player of the Year Award seven times in her first 11 years on tour.

"C" is for Casper,
and Crenshaw,
And Carner, JoAnne.
Their trophy collections
Would fill a large van.

BILLY CASPER posted 51 wins during a 20-year career (1956–1975) on the PGA Tour, the most memorable being his come-from-behind victory over Arnold Palmer in the 1966 U.S. Open at the Olympic Club in San Francisco, California.

Texas-born **BEN CRENSHAW** showed a deft hand with a putter when he captured Masters titles in 1984 and 1995.

JOANNE GUNDERSON CARNER was one of the best female amateurs ever, winning five U.S. Amateur crowns from 1957 through 1968 before a long and brilliant pro career. A large, hearty woman nicknamed "Big Momma" in her later years, she was a favorite of both fans and competitors.

"D" is for Demaret.

His wardrobe had blues, Greens, yellows, and reds, And bright pastel hues.

JIMMY DEMARET was famous for his peacock's wardrobe, which included hundreds of sweaters, slacks, and pairs of cleats. A genial former nightclub singer, he also entertained at many golfing parties, both official and impromptu. He shone on the course as well during the forties and fifties, winning—among other things—three Masters tournaments, in 1940, 1947, and 1950.

"E" is for eagle,

Golf's most famous score.
Gene Sarazen's double
Let him play one day more.

Jaunty **GENE SARAZEN** was a frequent champion in the twenties and thirties, when professional golf was just taking hold. In 1935, during the final round of the second Masters tournament at Augusta National Golf Club, he trailed Craig Wood by three shots with four holes to go. But on the 485-yard, par-4 15th hole, Sarazen made up all three with one swing, hitting a 220-yard, 4-wood shot onto the green and into the cup for a double-eagle 2. That forced a playoff the next day, which Sarazen won. The attention that the miracle shot brought to The Masters helped to make it an important event.

"F" is for "fore!"
Meaning you'd better duck,
Because if you don't,
You're pressing your luck!

"G" is for the green jacket,

The Masters champ's prize.
It always looks stylish,
No matter what size.

THE MASTERS TOURNAMENT BEGAN IN 1934 as an early spring stop between Florida and the Northeast for the touring pros, but it continually gained prominence until it ranked among golf's major events. Gene Sarazen's 1935 double eagle aided the process, but so did the flower-lined Augusta National Golf Club course, which matured into one of the world's most beautiful and challenging layouts. Also setting The Masters apart is the green jacket, emblematic of honorary membership in the exclusive club, which goes to each year's winner. He also gets a trophy and a large check, of course.

"H" is for Hogan,

Who had little to say. To opponents it was usually, "I think you're away."

"BANTAM" BEN HOGAN, from little Dublin, Texas, was anything but talkative, but his game spoke volumes. He achieved star status during the late thirties after struggling to conquer a hook during his early years as a pro, then was involved in an auto accident in 1949 that left him with permanent injuries. Nonetheless, he went on to play some of his best golf, adding three U.S. Open titles (in 1950, 1951, and 1953) to the one he'd won in 1948. His persistence in the face of adversity remains a stirring example of athletic courage.

"I" is for Irwin,

Who got better with age. Each year in his record Was a shiny new page.

HALE IRWIN, an All–Big Eight defensive back in his college days at the University of Colorado, won his third U.S. Open title in 1990 at the advanced age of 45, but his career only improved from there. He joined the Senior (now Champions) Tour in 1995, and his win total of 40 tournaments through 2004 became a record, as did his winnings of approximately $26.5 million. He has won the Senior PGA Championship four times.

"J" is for Bobby Jones,

Whose "Slam" was so grand That it lit up the game and Brought cheer to the land.

ROBERT TYRE JONES JR. was unquestionably the best golfer who never turned pro. A summer player who attended college throughout his championship days (he eventually earned degrees in engineering, English literature, and law), he won five U.S. Amateur titles, four U.S. Opens, three British Opens, and a British Amateur. He retired from competition in 1930 after capturing all four of those tournaments that same year—an unprecedented Grand Slam that roused Depression-era America and earned him a ticker-tape parade down Broadway Avenue in New York. In later life he practiced law, wrote about golf, and nurtured the Augusta National Golf Club, which he founded and helped design.

"K" is for Kite,

Who polished his specs,
Posted some birdies,
And cashed some big checks.

TOM KITE showed that short men (he stood 5'9") who wore glasses could also be golfing stars. He won 19 PGA tournaments, including the 1992 U.S. Open at the beautiful and treacherous Pebble Beach, California, course. He also played on seven U.S. Ryder Cup teams and was the nonplaying captain of the 1997 squad.

"L" is for "Lord By"—
Byron Nelson by name. His 11-win streak Highlighted his fame.

BYRON NELSON had a short professional golf career, but a brilliant one. Born in Fort Worth, Texas, he began winning soon after he turned pro in 1932 and got better from there. In 1945 he won 11 consecutive PGA Tour events and 18 overall—records that are unlikely to be broken. His winnings enabled him to achieve his ambition of owning a cattle ranch in his home state. He retired there after the 1946 season, but continued in the sport as a teacher and television commentator.

NANCY LOPEZ, from Torrance, California, was a leading light on the LPGA Tour for 15 years beginning in 1978. She won 48 times during her career, and her smiles drew fans to women's events.

"M" is for Mickelson,

Who swings from the left.
With a driver he's long,
With a wedge he is deft.

PHIL MICKELSON is right-handed, but learned to play golf left-handed as a child by mirroring his father's right-handed swing. He signaled his promise by winning the U.S. Amateur in 1990 and a PGA Tour event the next year—before he'd turned pro. His 20-win career's highlight was his triumph in the 2004 Masters tournament. His signature shot is the "plop shot," a soft, high wedge that stays just about where it lands. He's probably the best lefty ever to play the game.

"N" is for Nicklaus,

The best of the best. With wins in 20 majors, He leads all the rest.

It's widely agreed that **JACK NICKLAUS** was the best golfer ever. A big, sturdy man from Columbus, Ohio, he combined power with finesse. He turned professional in 1962 after winning two U.S. Amateur titles, and his first pro victory was that year's U.S. Open, where he defeated Arnold Palmer in a playoff. His 20 wins in major tournaments—the U.S. Amateur and Open, The Masters, British Open, and PGA Championship—over a 28-year period (1959–1986) are a record. He joined the Senior Tour in 1990, and quickly won all four majors on that circuit, too.

"O" is for Ouimet,

Barely more than a teen
When he defeated the Brits
In 1913.

FRANCIS OUIMET grew up across the street from The Country Club in Brookline, Massachusetts, where the 1913 U.S. Open Championship was staged. Although the 20-year-old had a good local reputation as an amateur, it was considered highly unlikely that he would win, especially since the field included the Englishmen Harry Vardon, the best player of his era, and Ted Ray, the reigning British Open champ. Still, Ouimet, trailed by his 10-year-old caddie Eddie Lowery, tied those two after the 72 holes of regulation play and defeated them soundly in the next day's 18-hole playoff. Ouimet's victory is credited with beginning America's long period of golf domination.

"P" is for Palmer,

Who went for the pin,
Hit an iron shot stiff,
Then rammed the putt in.

ARNOLD PALMER wasn't the best golfer of his day (Jack Nicklaus was), but his bold playing style and engaging personality made him one of the game's all-time fan favorites. He won seven major titles, including four Masters (in 1958, 1960, 1962, and 1964) and many others worldwide. He's best known as the commander of "Arnie's Army," the legion of spectators that sprang up to cheer him wherever he appeared. His magnetism helped to propel the PGA Tour to new popular and financial heights.

"Q" is for "quiet!"
With no "ifs" or "buts"
When the golfers get ready
To line up their putts.

"R" is for Chi Chi Rodriguez,

Who'd chuckle with glee,
Turn his putter around,
And slash out a "Z."

JUAN ANTONIO "CHI CHI" RODRIGUEZ is another golfer who made his mark mainly through popular appeal. Born poor in Rio Piedras, Puerto Rico, he boxed in the streets for money as a boy, and his first golf club was a branch from a guava tree. He learned the game as a caddy, and won nine PGA Tour events from 1963 through 1979. His real success was on the Senior Tour, where his 22 wins included the 1986 PGA Senior Championship. Fans loved the way he hurled his slender body into his drives and engaged in mock swordplay with his putter after sinking a long one.

"S" is for Snead,
Whose huge title array
Never made up for
The one that got away.

SAM SNEAD was a leading PGA Tour player over a 30-year period (1937–1967), during which he posted a record 81 victories. A strongly built man who was an excellent all-around athlete as a youth in Hot Springs, Virginia, his self-taught swing was long regarded as the game's smoothest and most powerful. He won seven major crowns and was superb in match play, but probably is better known for his four runner-up finishes in the U.S. Open—the one big title to elude him. He was a founder of the PGA Senior Tour and a prolific and amusing author of instructional golf books.

"T" is for Trevino,

Who learned golf on a range.
After he'd won some big ones,
Folks stopped finding that strange.

LEE TREVINO was raised in a Mexican-American family in East Dallas, Texas, and learned his game on that city's driving ranges and hardscrabble municipal courses. He emerged with steady nerves and a low ball-hitting style that served him well on the manicured acres on which the big-time pro tournaments were staged. He won the U.S. Open in 1968, his third year out, and went on to compete with the likes of Jack Nicklaus, Tom Watson, and South African star Gary Player in the game's premier events, winning more than his share. His joking manner led his more devoted followers to dub themselves "Lee's Fleas."

"U" is for the
U.S. Open,

A big tourney, and more.
It reminds the game's heroes
That par's a good score.

THE U.S. OPEN WAS FIRST PLAYED IN 1895 and, except for six years during the World Wars (1917–1918 and 1942–1945), has been contested annually. Besides being the national tournament of the world's foremost golfing nation, it's known for the challenging nature of the courses on which it is played. The U.S. Golf Association, which stages it, always picks a difficult layout and makes it harder by narrowing the fairways, speeding the greens, and letting the rough grow long. Players often mutter about the tournament's severity, but they also agree that it's one that only the best players can win.

"V" is for Vijay,

Who turned into a champ
On the practice tee, wearing
A cap with a lamp.

VIJAY SINGH, from the island of Fiji in the Southwest Pacific Ocean, joined the PGA Tour in 1993 and quickly became known for the long hours he put in on the practice tee, often extending his workouts until after the sun had set. His hard work began to pay off in earnest when he won the 1998 PGA Championship and vaulted to number two on that year's money list. His career crested during a 2004 season in which he won nine times and secured the world's top ranking.

HARRY VARDON, an Englishman, was the greatest star of golf's early competitive days, winning six British Opens between 1896 and 1914. He invented the overlapping grip most golfers use today.

"W" is for Tiger Woods,

For whom golf was like breathing.
He became a big star
Before he finished teething.

Prodded by his father, a former army officer, **ELDRICK "TIGER" WOODS** was a golfing prodigy from infancy. He putted on a television show at age two, and the next year shot a 48 on a full-sized nine-hole course. Growing tall, strong, and limber, he turned pro at age 21 in 1996 after winning just about every national age-group and amateur title he sought. He was a tour winner his first year out. By the end of 2004 he'd won all four of the game's majors at least once and had spent more than six years as number one in the official World Golf Ranking.

"X" marks "the shot"

Off a Lew Worsham swing. When it went in the cup, The tour's fortunes took wing.

IN 1953 PROMOTER GEORGE S. MAY OFFERED A $25,000 PRIZE—the largest up to that time—to the winner of his tournament on the Tam O'Shanter course outside Chicago, Illinois. Lew Worsham, a veteran pro, came to the final hole of that event needing a birdie 3 to tie for the lead and force a playoff for the big check. Instead, his 109-yard wedge second shot rolled into the hole, giving him an eagle and an outright victory. The sensational shot was televised live to a 15-state hookup, golf's largest to that point. It sharply increased fan interest and promoted wider TV coverage and larger purses for PGA Tour events.

Another memorable shot was TOM WATSON's chip-in birdie 2 on the 71st hole of the 1982 U.S. Open at Pebble Beach, which clinched his victory over Jack Nicklaus in the event.

"Y" is for yardage,

The game's thrilling new race.
Using moon-shot materials,
Players conquer space.

"Z" is for Zaharias,

Of Olympic track fame.
Women's golf got a boost
When she took up the game.

MILDRED ELLA "BABE" DIDRIKSON ZAHARIAS starred in basketball, softball, and track-and-field as a girl. She won gold medals in the 80-meter hurdles and javelin throw at the 1932 Olympic Games in Los Angeles. Looking for other outlets, she took up golf at age 21. She quickly excelled and made it her livelihood. She played mostly exhibitions at first, then joined with a handful of other female players to start the LPGA Tour in 1950. She won 31 of that circuit's first 128 events, and her popularity buoyed the new enterprise. She died of cancer in 1956 at age 42, but not before she was voted the best female athlete of the first half of the 20th century.

"A" is for St. Andrews

"B" is for Ballesteros

"C" is for Carner,
Casper, and Crenshaw

"D" is for Demaret

"F" is for fore

"H" is for Hogan

"I" is for Irwin

"J" is for Jones

"K" is for Kite

"L" is for Lord By

"L" is also for Lopez

"M" is for Mickelson

"N" is for Nicklaus

"O" is for Ouimet

"P" is for Palmer

"R" is for Rodriguez

"S" is for Snead

"T" is for Trevino

"V" is for Vijay

"W" is for Woods

"Z" is for Zaharias

"A" is for Artist

"W" is for Writer

Library of Congress Control Number: 2005901147

This book is available in quantity at special discounts for your group or organization. For further information, contact:

Triumph Books
542 S. Dearborn St., Suite 750
Chicago, Illinois 60605
(312) 939-3330
Fax (312) 663-3557

Printed in Hong Kong
ISBN-13: 978-1-57243-751-6
ISBN-10: 1-57243-751-0